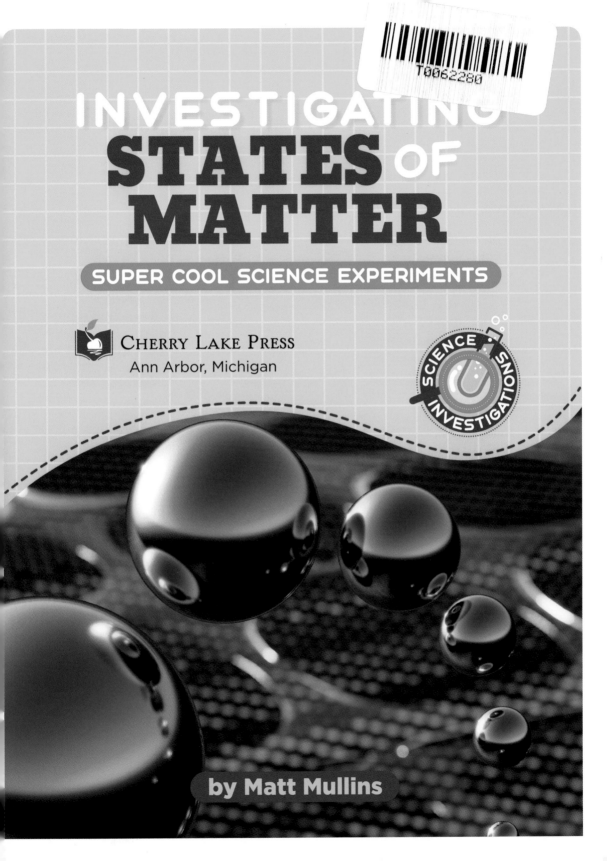

# INVESTIGATING STATES OF MATTER

## SUPER COOL SCIENCE EXPERIMENTS

CHERRY LAKE PRESS
Ann Arbor, Michigan

SCIENCE INVESTIGATION

by Matt Mullins

## CHERRY LAKE PRESS

Published in the United States of America by
Cherry Lake Publishing Group
Ann Arbor, Michigan
www.cherrylakepublishing.com

Reading Adviser: Beth Walker Gambro, MS, Ed., Reading Consultant, Yorkville, IL

Content Editor: Robert Wolffe, EdD,
Professor of Teacher Education, Bradley University, Peoria, Illinois

Book Designer: Ed Morgan of Bowerbird Books

Grateful acknowledgment to Deborah Simon, Department of Chemistry, Whitman College

Photo Credits: cover and title page, 4, 6, 7, 16, 19, 20, 23, 24, 27, 29,freepik.com; 5, 9, 10, 11, 12, 13, 14, 15, 17, 18, 21, 22, 25, 26, 28 The Design Lab.

**Cherry Lake Press** is an imprint of Cherry Lake Publishing Group.

Library of Congress Cataloging-in-Publication Data has been filed and is available at catalog.loc.gov

Printed in the United States of America
Corporate Graphics

**A Note to Parents and Teachers:** Please review the instructions for these experiments before your children do them. Be sure to help them with any experiments you do not think they can safely conduct on their own.

**A Note to Kids:** Be sure to ask an adult for help with these experiments when you need it. Always put your safety first!

Note from Publisher: Websites change regularly, and their future contents are outside of our control. Supervise children when conducting any recommended online searches for extended learning opportunities.

# CONTENTS

Science Matters!. . . . . . . . . . . . . . . . . . . . . . . . .4

Getting Started . . . . . . . . . . . . . . . . . . . . . . . .5

Experiment 1: . . . . . . . . . . . . . . . . . . . . . . . .8
Matter Bonds

Experiment 2: . . . . . . . . . . . . . . . . . . . . . . . 12
Solids, Liquids, and Gases

Experiment 3: . . . . . . . . . . . . . . . . . . . . . . . 16
Matter Takes Up Space

Experiment 4: . . . . . . . . . . . . . . . . . . . . . . . 20
Density and Weight

Experiment 5: . . . . . . . . . . . . . . . . . . . . . . . 24
Matter Is Cool

Experiment 6: . . . . . . . . . . . . . . . . . . . . . . . 28
Do It Yourself!

Glossary . . . . . . . . . . . . . . . . . 30
For More Information . . . . . . . 31
Index. . . . . . . . . . . . . . . . . . . . . 32
About the Author . . . . . . . . . 32

# Science MATTERS!

What exactly is matter? Matter is anything that has weight. Think of some examples around you such as the chair you're sitting in or the book you're reading. All stuff is matter. Did you know matter comes in three different forms called **states**? These are: solids, liquids, and gases. Solids and liquids are pretty easy to identify. Gases are harder to distinguish because they're often invisible. However, like solids and liquids, gases also have weight. Scientists study all types of matter down to their smallest unit—the **atom**. They study how atoms bind together as **molecules**.

Solid

Gas

Liquid

# Getting STARTED

In this book, you will learn how to study states of matter like a scientist! Scientists learn about things by coming up with questions and carrying out experiments. They write down their **observations**. You will learn how to create your own experiments, too! You don't need a fancy lab to get started. You can use items you already have at home. In the process, you'll make a lot of fascinating discoveries about matter.

When scientists design experiments, they often use the scientific method. What is the scientific method? It's a step-by-step process to answer specific questions. The steps don't always follow the same pattern. However, the scientific method often works like this:

**STEP ONE:** A scientist gathers the facts and makes observations about one particular thing.

**STEP TWO:** The scientist comes up with a question that is not answered by the observations and facts.

**STEP THREE:** The scientist creates a **hypothesis**. This is a statement about what the scientist thinks might be the answer to the question.

**STEP FOUR:** The scientist tests the hypothesis by designing an experiment to see whether the hypothesis is correct. Then the scientist carries out the experiment and writes down what happens.

**STEP FIVE:** The scientist draws a **conclusion** based on the result of the experiment. The conclusion might be that the hypothesis is correct. Sometimes, though, the hypothesis is not correct. In that case, the scientist might develop a new hypothesis and another experiment.

In the following experiments, we'll see the scientific method in action. You'll be thinking and experimenting like a scientist. Your home will become your very own laboratory! You will test hypotheses and come to conclusions. By the end of the book, you'll know a lot about states of matter. Are you ready, young scientist? Let's get started!

# · EXPERIMENT 1 ·

## Matter Bonds

We know that matter is made up of atoms. And one or more atoms of any kind that stick together, or bond, are called molecules. Some molecules are multiple atoms of the same kind. An oxygen molecule is made up of two oxygen atoms. That's why it's often shown as $O^2$. Other atoms and molecules form compounds. Water is a compound. A water molecule, or $H^2O$, combines two hydrogen atoms with one oxygen atom. Molecules bind with other molecules to make up a substance.

Let's investigate! Have you ever noticed that a drop of water looks slightly rounded at top? The water molecules are attracted to each other. The attraction creates something called surface tension. If the attraction is strong, a thin skin forms on the surface, holding the molecules together. Do all liquids act like this? Are their molecules as strongly attached to each other? Our hypothesis can be: **Liquid molecules are all attracted to each other as strongly as water molecules are.**

# Here's what you'll need:

- 3 small glasses
- Water
- Dish soap
- A plastic spoon
- A dish towel
- Rubbing alcohol
- 2 medicine droppers

# · INSTRUCTIONS ·

1. Fill 2 glasses 3/4 full of water. Add several drops of dish soap to 1 glass. Stir well with the spoon.

2. Add more water up to the rim of both glasses. Use the towel to dry off the sides of the glasses.

3. Fill the third glass to the rim with rubbing alcohol. Ask an adult for help. Be very careful when using rubbing alcohol. Be sure not to get any in your mouth or eyes.

4. Fill 1 of the droppers with water. Drip water into the glass that's filled with plain water. See if you can make the water bulge up in a dome above the rim of the glass. Write down what you observe.

5. Fill the same dropper with soapy water. Drip soapy drops into the glass with soapy water. Can you make the soapy water bulge up by adding enough drops? Record what you see.

6. Fill the other dropper with rubbing alcohol. Add drops to the glass of rubbing alcohol. Can you make that liquid bulge? Write down your observations.

# · CONCLUSION ·

What happened when you added drops and the liquids reached over the rim of the glasses? Did all of the liquids behave in the same way?

The force of attraction between molecules varies. The bond is stronger in some substances than in others. Surface tension helps the molecules of certain liquids stay together. They form a dome instead of spilling over the glass. Soap weakens surface tension. Also, gravity becomes stronger than the attraction between molecules when you add lots of drops. Does this explain your results? Would you conclude that the molecules of certain liquids bonded better than others? Was our hypothesis correct?

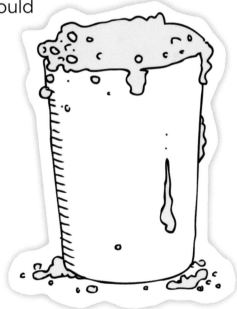

# ·EXPERIMENT 2·

## Solids, Liquids, and Gases

Solids have molecules with less energy and can hold onto each other tightly. Molecules are always attracted to one another. Their attraction keeps them in place. As they get more energy, they can move around more and overcome the pull. In a liquid, molecules can move enough to slip past one another. But the attraction still keeps them grouped together. In a gas, there is so much energy that the attraction can no longer keep the molecules together. They move around freely.

A substance's state of matter, then, is determined by how much energy its molecules have to move. The extra energy weakens molecules' attraction to each other. Can a substance's state of matter change? Can more energy make molecules move more? How can we give a substance more energy?

Heat is a form of energy. Can we use heat to change states of matter? Let's investigate by developing a hypothesis. Here is one option: **By adding heat, the state of water can be changed from a solid to a liquid to a gas.**

# Here's what you'll need:

- Ice cubes
- 1-gallon (3.8 liters) resealable plastic freezer bag
- A microwave oven
- An adult helper

# · INSTRUCTIONS ·

1. Place 2 ice cubes in the freezer bag. Lay the bag flat on a counter. Flatten out the bag before sealing it so there's very little air in it.

2. Place the bag in the microwave. Ask an adult to run the microwave for 20 seconds. Watch through the microwave oven window as the ice heats. Have the adult continue to run the microwave for 20-second periods until the ice has completely melted.

3. Have the adult run the microwave for more 20-second intervals to see if you can change the liquid into a gas. Do you notice a change in the bag? Write down your observations.

# ·CONCLUSION·

How much time does it take for the ice to melt into a liquid? As you continue to heat it, what happens to the liquid? What happens to the bag? Does the bag stay the same size? Does it expand? Why or why not?

Ice is a solid. The water molecules are attracted to one another and slow down. Heating the ice causes the molecules to gain energy and move more. If the molecules gain enough energy, they slide past one another. The solid becomes a liquid. Adding more heat to the liquid causes the molecules to move even faster. The molecules eventually gain enough energy to pass beyond the molecules that are at the liquid's surface. These molecules rise up into the air as a gas or water vapor. This process is called **evaporation**. If your bag expanded, could this vapor be the reason why? Was your hypothesis correct?

# Matter Takes Up Space

Matter *always* takes up space. A solid keeps its shape no matter where you put it. A liquid takes the shape of whatever container you put it in. Gas also fills up whatever container it is in. For example, if you put gas in a balloon, it will be shaped like a balloon.

If you had a big bottle of water and tried to pour it into a little bottle, what would happen? Would the liquid overflow? What if you tried to do the same with gas? **Volume** is the amount of space that gas or another form of matter takes up.

Do liquids and gases react differently to changes in the spaces they take up? Think about water and air. Our hypothesis could be: **Water of a certain volume can't be contained in a space with a smaller volume, but air of a certain volume can be contained in a space that has a smaller volume.**

# Here's what you'll need:

- 2 identical empty dish soap bottles with caps
- Water
- Air

# · INSTRUCTIONS ·

**1.** Fill one of the bottles to the top with water. Screw the cap on tightly.

**2.** Open the other bottle to let air in. Screw the cap on tightly.

**3.** Squeeze the bottle filled with water. What happens? Can you squeeze it very much? Write down your observations.

**4.** Hold the water bottle over the sink with the nozzle on top. Open the nozzle. Squeeze the bottle. What did you observe this time?

**5.** Make sure the nozzle of the bottle filled with air is closed. Hold your finger over the nozzle and squeeze the bottle. Are you able to make it smaller?

# CONCLUSION

What did you observe? Could you feel the bottle of water resist, or push against, your hand as you tried to squeeze it with the cap closed? Could you squeeze the water into a smaller space? What did the water do when you opened the cap and squeezed? Did creating a space for the water to go allow you to make the space in the bottle smaller? How did the air in the second bottle react to the squeezing? Were you able to squeeze the bottle even though the cap was closed? What does this tell you about the ability of air to be **compressed**? There is more space between gas molecules than the molecules of a liquid. Does this help explain your findings? What can you conclude?

Think about the volume of air the next time you crush a plastic bottle before recycling it!

# Density and Weight

All matter—solids, liquids, and gases—has weight. All matter also has density. But density is not the same thing as weight. Picture 1 pound (0.45 kilogram) of cotton candy and 1 pound of gold. They both weigh 1 pound. But it would take a small bag to hold the gold and a huge bag to hold the cotton candy. That's because gold is denser than cotton candy. Gold takes up much less space than an equal weight of cotton candy. Think of density as the amount of mass or molecules packed into a certain space.

Different types of matter have different densities. We learned about solids, but what about liquids? Let's use three common liquids: rubbing alcohol, water, and cooking oil. Here are two hypotheses that can be tested with the same experiment:

**Hypothesis #1: Rubbing alcohol is denser than cooking oil.**

**Hypothesis #2: Water is denser than rubbing alcohol.**

# Here's what you'll need:

- A glass jar
- Rubbing alcohol
- Blue and red food coloring
- A plastic spoon
- A funnel with a long tip
- Vegetable oil
- Water
- A drinking glass

**1.** Fill 1/4 of the jar with rubbing alcohol. Ask an adult for help. Add several drops of blue food coloring to the alcohol, and stir with the spoon.

**2.** Put the funnel over the mouth of the jar. The tip of the funnel should be long enough to extend down toward the bottom of the jar.

**3.** Pour in vegetable oil until it fills another 1/4 of the jar. Remove the funnel. Which liquid is on top? Which is on the bottom?

**4.** Put some water in a glass. Add several drops of red food coloring.

**5.** Pour the red water through the funnel into the jar. Stop when the jar is about 1/4 full.

# CONCLUSION

Observe the liquid layers. Do you see three bands of liquid? Which is on top? Which is on the bottom? Which is in the center? The one on the bottom is the densest. The one on the top is the least dense. Is alcohol denser or less dense than cooking oil? Is water more or less dense than alcohol? Is water more or less dense than oil? Did you prove your hypotheses?

## FACTS!

Water has some strange qualities. It is a special type of matter that is denser as a liquid than it is as a solid. Most stuff is denser as a solid, such as gold. Drop solid gold into liquid gold and it sinks right to the bottom. But add ice to a glass of water and it floats!

# EXPERIMENT 5

## Matter Is Cool

The freezing point of a liquid is the temperature at which it turns into a solid. For water, that's 32° Fahrenheit (0° Celsius). When a liquid becomes solid, the attraction between the molecules is strong. So the freezing point is the stage at which the bond between molecules keeps all the molecules in place.

Did you know we can use science to **supercool** a liquid? In other words, we can cool it so fast that even below its freezing point, it stays liquid!

Scientists know that a supercooled liquid needs a little extra energy, or a disturbance of some kind, to suddenly freeze. Could this concept be applied to water? Let's try it. Here is one option for a hypothesis: **Water can be supercooled and needs to be disturbed before it can freeze.**

# Here's what you'll need:

- 6 bottles of distilled water or high-quality spring water
- A refrigerator
- A freezer
- A kitchen towel

# · INSTRUCTIONS ·

1. Chill the water bottles in the refrigerator overnight.

2. Gently remove the bottles from the fridge. Examine them carefully. You only want water that does not have bubbles in it.

3. Choose 3 bottles without bubbles in them. Place them in the freezer carefully to avoid making any bubbles in the water. They should be set in the freezer in an upright position for 3 hours.

4. After 3 hours, remove the bottles of water. Gently place them on a countertop. Tip the bottles a bit to make sure they are still liquid. Very gently wipe off the outside of the bottles with the kitchen towel.

5. Take a bottle and tap it on the counter. What happens?

6. Repeat the process with the other 2 bottles.

# ·CONCLUSION·

What happened when you disturbed the water by banging the bottle on a hard surface? Did it freeze? If so, how does this happen? In a properly supercooled bottle of water, the liquid will turn to ice at one spot when you disturb it. The ice will quickly spread. The whole bottle will turn to ice right before your eyes! Amazing, isn't it?

## FACTS!

The science behind supercooling is complicated. Adding energy by disturbing the water and making molecules bump into one another is not the only reason the water freezes. Molecules also need to form as solids around something. That something might be an extra-cool spot on the container or a bubble created by shaking. That's why the experiment doesn't work if the water has a bubble in it before supercooling or if the water isn't very pure.

## ·EXPERIMENT 6·

# Do It Yourself!

It's time to continue learning by designing your own experiments. Start in your kitchen. Try determining the temperature at which liquid water turns to gas. What would your hypothesis be? How would you run an experiment to find the answer? What kitchen tools would you use?

Or you could mix a solid such as salt with a liquid such as water. Could you find a way to get the salt back after mixing it in water? How could your knowledge of states of matter—and water in particular—help you? What would your experiment be?

You've learned a lot about different states of matter. You've even found a way to make water super cool! Experiments may not always turn out as you planned. But by thinking like a scientist, you've gained some important tools that will help you learn more about the world around you. And what a world it is!

## FACTS!

Now that you can think like a scientist, so many things are possible! Scientists rarely work alone. So consider designing an experiment with a friend. Work together to follow the steps you learned in this book.

# Glossary

**atom (AT-uhm)** the smallest part of an element that still has the properties of the element

**compressed (kuhm-PREST)** condensed; pressed into less space

**conclusion (kuhn-KLOO-zhuhn)** a final decision, thought, or opinion

**evaporation (ih-vah-puh-RAY-shuhn)** the process in which a liquid changes to a gas or vapor

**hypothesis (hy-POTH-uh-sihss)** a logical guess about what will happen in an experiment

**molecules (MOL-uh-kyoolz)** the smallest forms of a material that have the chemical properties of the material and are made up of two or more atoms

**observations (ob-zur-VAY-shuhnz)** things that are seen or noticed with one's senses

**states (STAYTS)** forms of matter

**supercool (soo-pur-KOOL)** to lower the temperature of something below its freezing point without it becoming solid

**volume (VOL-yuhm)** the amount of space taken up by a three-dimensional object or substance

# For More Information

**BOOKS**

Baker, Laura. *Physics for Curious Kids*. London: Arcturus, 2022.

Squire, Ann O. *Physical Science: Matter*. New York: Scholastic, 2019.

*Super Simple Physics*. New York: DK Publishing, 2021.

**WEBSITES**

Explore these online sources with an adult:

Britannica Kids: States of Matter

NASA: States of Matter

PBS Kids: States of Matter

PBS Learning Media: States of Matter

# Index

atoms, 4, 8
attraction forces, 8, 11, 12–13, 15, 24

bonds, 8, 10–11, 12–13, 24

changes, states of matter, 12–15, 24–27, 28
compounds, 8
compression, 19
conclusions
  of experiments, 11, 15, 19, 23, 27
  scientific method, 6, 7
cooling and heating, 12–15, 24–27, 28

density, 20, 22–23

experiments
  scientific method, 5, 6, 7
  on states of matter, 8–11, 12–15, 16–19,
    20–23, 24–27, 28–29
  supplies, 9, 13, 17, 21, 25

facts
  natural phenomena, 4, 23, 27
  scientific method, 6, 7

gases, 4, 12
  chemical bonds, 12–13, 15
  experiments, 12–15, 16–19, 28
  volume and shape, 16–17, 19

heating and cooling, 12–15, 24–27, 28
hypotheses
  matter-related, 8, 11, 13, 15, 17, 20, 23,
    24, 28
  scientific method, 6, 7

liquids, 4, 12
  chemical bonds, 8, 11, 12, 15, 24
  density and weight, 20, 23
  experiments, 8–11, 12–15, 16–19, 20–23,
    24–27, 28
  volume and shape, 16–17, 19

matter, 4, 8, 12, 16, 20
molecules, 4, 12–14, 20, 24
  in gases, 12–13, 15, 19
  in liquids, 8, 11, 12–13, 15, 19, 24, 27
  in solids, 12, 15, 24, 27

observations
  about matter, 4, 8, 15, 16, 19, 20, 24
  experiment activities, 10–11, 14–15, 18–19,
    22–23, 26–27
  scientific method, 5, 6

scientific method, 5–7
solids, 4, 12
  chemical bonds, 12, 15, 24
  density and weight, 20, 23
  experiments, 12–15, 24–27, 28
  volume and shape, 16
solubility, 29
supercooling, 24, 27
supplies, experiments, 9, 13, 17, 21, 25
surface tension, 8, 11

volume, 16–17, 19

water
  chemical bonds, 8, 11, 12–13, 15, 24, 27
  experiments, 8–11, 12–15, 20–23, 24–27,
    28
  special qualities, 23
  weight, 20, 22–23

# About the Author

Matt Mullins holds a master's degree in the history of science. He lives in Madison, Wisconsin, with his wife and son. Matt writes about science and technology, food, and other topics that interest him.